I Am Me

INSIDE THE MIND OF AN ADDICT

by Angelise Tomasino

DORRANCE
PUBLISHING CO
EST. 1920
PITTSBURGH, PENNSYLVANIA 15238

Dorrance Publishing Co
585 Alpha Drive
Suite 103
Pittsburgh, PA 15238
Visit our website at *www.dorrancebookstore.com*

ISBN: 978-1-6461-0979-1
eISBN: 978-1-6461-0268-6

Dedication

This book is dedicated to my grandparents, Mary T. and Big Lou. I love you both. I hope I'm making you proud.

I See Her

I see her. I see the little girl with tossled hair, messy from being asleep. I see her make her way towards the bathroom, eager to get back to her bed. Sleeping is peaceful for her. Then I see her stop short. I see her eyes fill with a feeling of horror no child could possibly process at that age. I feel it now. That deep-seeded fear. That sick, dark hole that became imprinted into her soul. I see her watching her father staring at the TV with a woman being raped by multiple men. I see him leaning forward toward the TV to get a better look as he presses rewind over and over and over.

I then see the wall that shoots up. I feel the strength of the determination to protect that innocent little girl. For her mind's natural instinct from the minute she was brought into this world is to protect her from what cause anguish or pain or danger. I see it encompass her entire heart and soul, but she does not. She doesn't even know it exists. She doesn't know this would begin her downward slope into a Hell she will create, which will ultimately leave a trail of destruction behind her she couldn't even see.

I see her come to a dangerous conclusion in her vulnerable mind. She didn't understand what she saw on the TV, but she saw it made her father happy even though the lady was screaming. *So people watching other people scared is supposed to be a happy thing*, she guesses. Back to bed she goes, oblivious to the trauma her soul just experienced.

I watch as she tries to win her father's love and affection. Nothing she does ever seems to do it. Being scared of him is something that comes as natural as breathing to her now, but she is also dying for him to pay attention to her, and to look at her without indifference. She doesn't know what she's doing to make him hate her so much. All she feels is that he does. I feel both the terror and emptiness filling her heart—a heart simply needing the one man in her life who should've always loved her.

I see a few years go by. Then I see her being raped by a man who was void of anything good or human, for that matter. I feel the pressure of him on top of her chest. That made it impossible to imagine him not being there. I see him threatening to do the same to her younger sisters. The plaid shirt, and the disgusting smell of sweat and Old Spice, his labored breathing into her right ear. Then I feel her mind concentrating on one sole goal, the only thing that could bring any form of joy to her heart at the moment. I feel her desire to strangle this monster and watch the life drain out of him. I see her picturing the light go out in his eyes and taking his demonic heart with him to Hell where he belongs.

Then I see her deciding to end this, deciding she has been torn apart enough, deciding no man will ever hurt her again. I walk with her toward the kitchen to grab the biggest knife she can find. I watch her make a hole in the bottom of the mattress on the top bunk of her bunk bed. I feel her promise herself she will stop this. I see her slide the knife into the hole, blade first with the handle out, just enough for her to be able to get to it quickly, but not for it to be obvious or seen by anyone else. Then I see her wait. Wait for the next time. She knows it will come, and it does, but she's ready. He doesn't see it coming. She reaches up and pulls the knife out swiftly. Before he realizes it, she has the blade to his neck, shoving as hard as she can into his throat with the flat side. I hear her tell him in that moment she is in control of him living or dying. She is the reason his heart is still beating. All she has to do is flick her wrist to switch the position of the knife for his pathetic life to be over. It is effective. He never touches her again.

BOOM.

Another wall went up surrounding the existing one. See, what she realizes in that moment is she saved herself. All alone, no support, and it shows her she doesn't need anybody to look out for her. If she wants to be safe and protected, she is the only one capable of doing so.

I can see her—a little older, in junior high school. I can see her struggling. She is not aware of it. She has all of her focus on doing well in school and doing what she needs to in order for her to live her life happily. I can see how tired she is from carrying the weight of what has been in her heart for quite some time now. She still believes in happiness and love, even though she isn't getting any from the ones who were supposed to love her unconditionally. I watch her throw herself into her academics, sports, and reading—anything that could aid in reaching her goal to get away from the two homes from which she is passed back and forth, each with their own individual Hells.

I see her muster up the courage to finally tell someone about the trauma she has gone through. It keeps getting closer and closer to the surface, and she wants it gone. She knows she has to be brave. I watch as she begins to tell this person about the demons that ripped away her innocence. Then I see the person stop her from talking and not wanting to hear the rest. I witness the shift in this poor girl's eyes and the switch to a very hardened, different way of seeing things.

BOOM.

I watch a third wall form around her heart. This one is a particularly important one. I see her make the conscious decision to now never let *anyone* hurt her again, male or female. I watch as her remaining hope for happiness and love drifts away as she freely relinquishes them both, no longer believing in anything else but pain and survival. She grows to accept pain is a way of showing you you're still alive, so it's a strong factor in survival. I see her welcoming that pain into every inch of her being and becoming comfortable with it.

I see what the years following that decision bring. I watch her fall hard into drugs, sex, and partying. She eventually quits high school altogether because she can't care less about anything that may help her. I see the pain she both carries and inflicts upon others. I see the darkness in her, the depth of it hidden behind her eyes.

I see her move forward into adulthood. She gets a job at a restaurant, and in time, marries the owner, who is far older than she. I see her being manipulated and used and talked down to in the years to come. I watch her chase him, dying to be loved, and I see him torment her time and time again. As long as she is doing, saying, acting, and living exactly how he wants her to, he loves her, but if she wasn't, he shows her nothing but hate and indifference.

I watch her get abused throughout the period of this relationship. I can see the cycle of it all and the point it brings her to. I see her at the doctor with a torn meniscus and an enormous cyst in her knee. I watch the doctor prescribe her a prescription for vicodin to help with the pain. I watch her go almost two years straight taking them every day. It becomes a part of her normal schedule. Wake up, go to the bathroom, take the pills and go on about her day. I see her finally get the surgery done. She takes the last pill a few days later and heads in to work. I watch her soon become violently ill—shaking from pain, sweating incessantly, both throwing up and shitting at the same time. I see the moment in her eyes she realizes what this must be. She panics because there's so much she has to do, so many people depending on her, or watching her every move waiting for her to screw up so they will have something else to use against her. She doesn't have the time to go through a withdrawal process. I watch her, with her mind locked in survival mode, make the decision to get some more, however possible, just until she finishes everything she's responsible for first. She needs to get these pills. Otherwise, she can't be whoever everyone else needs her to be.

BOOM.

Another wall circumferences itself right in front of the other walls. This one's main purpose is to shut out reason and truth so denial and more bad decisions than she knows to be possible can get comfortable, right next to the pain, anger, and the self-loathing tendencies she already had.

I see her with what she thinks her happiness depends upon. I watch her fall in love with those pills. They are everything to her. She will stop at nothing to make sure she is never without. They make her happy. They help her pass out at the end of the long day instead of trying to sleep on her own, terrified of the nightmares that will surely come. She will do anything for them, seeing as they are the only source of peace she has. I watch as the years go by as she willingly destroys her body so she is not able to feel anything real. I watch her trade her humanity for numbness. I watch her tolerance grow higher and higher. Some days, at her worst, she will take forty to fifty pills a day, ten at a time. I watch her once healthy, beautiful body waste away. She keeps moving, though. I see the day she looks and admits to herself she has a problem, and just as quickly as the notion comes to be, I watch it be buried. She can handle this on her own, just like she always has.

I watch her handle it. I watch her cut back, wean herself off, and quit taking the pain pills hundreds of times. I watch how it pushes her farther and farther down into her crushed existence each time she fails. I see her screaming for help internally, almost incessantly, but without seeing a possibility for actually doing so verbally. I watch as her addiction morphs her into a person unrecognizable.

She breaks free from the miserable marriage she's in. I watch her bask in the sense of freedom and relief she feels. I can see the determination on her face to change her life around. She has a fresh, brand-new start with no one holding her back.

Time moves forward a bit. I see her. I see her doing worse things, stealing from people she loves in order to keep her life together. I watch her lie and manipulate and hurt many, many people. I feel her inner anguish. The self-loathing. The self-hatred. The desire to just fucking die already. She despises the things she's doing. I watch her justify to herself she *has* to keep taking the pills. She now has the love of her life and a son to take care of and be there for. The sickness that would overcome her from quitting would be terrifying and debilitating in every sense, and that simply wasn't a possibility. I watch her tell herself for the thousandth time as soon as she takes care of a few things, she'll stop. She doesn't even realize the damage she's unintentionally doing. She thinks she's doing what she needs to for those she loves. She doesn't see each pill she takes pushes her farther and farther away from them, but she feels the distance—feels it but doesn't know where it's coming from. She feels it and works even harder at trying to please everyone. The pain from this is evident in her eyes. This she knows from staring back at her own reflection thousands of times. No one else sees it though. She feels alone, even with the ones she loves the most surrounding her.

I watch as her actions and choices catch up to her. I watch her be charged with forgery from stealing a prescription pad from a doctor's office along with possession of a controlled substance. I see her go through withdrawal in jail, fight for the toilet with her cellmate who's also going through withdrawal. I see her lying on the dirty floor of the jail covered in waste and vomit.

I see her in the weeks and months to follow. I see her slowly get clean. Get her demons out of her body. I watch as she fights day after day after day, never faulting or giving up. I see in her eyes a clarity, a sense of peace. I see her acknowledge while she still has work to do on herself, she is in a far better place than she was at the beginning of her eight-month sentence.

I watch as she rides home the day she is released. I feel her joy, her happiness, to be back with her family. I watch her acknowledge a small, tiny voice in the back of her mind telling her she needs more time in recovery before she goes home. I see her slap that thought with a force so strong I tremble in its intensity. She refuses to listen to anything other than going home, having no clue that while she may be clean physically, she still very much had the addict's mentality. This choice to go home makes her so happy, so fulfilled, until a couple weeks go by and that darkness, loneliness, and lack of self-worth return. I feel her feelings. The sadness. The feeling of failing once again. I feel her fighting against the urge to use almost every second of every day. I watch her strive forward with determination, but losing faith and hope in herself as time goes on. She goes on to have a beautiful baby girl the following summer. I see pure joy and love radiate from her. She doesn't see it.

BOOM.

She doesn't see until she changes her addict/street mentality, nothing else will. She doesn't realize this type of mentality can kill you just as much as the pills can, possibly quicker. At this point, small, but strong, walls are shooting up from every failure, every bad thought or worry. There are now so many walls of all shapes and sizes surrounding her heart, it seems impossible to ever get to again. I see her dying inside a little more every day until the inevitable happens. I see her stare at herself in the mirror and the moment she succumbs to her demon. I watch as she spends almost one thousand dollars in a week's time from buying pain pills. I see her hate herself with a vengeance with a strong sense of anger keeping the hate afloat. Then I see her acknowledge she is angry with herself. I see the exact moment she becomes tired of her own shit.

I watch as she confesses to her partner she has relapsed. I see the tears of shame, guilt, and sadness pour out of her. I see the man she loves with her whole heart take her in his arms. I see her feeling broken and so disappointed in herself. She has done the one thing she swore she would never do again—let down the people she loves.

And then I see her do something I have never seen her do. I watch as she hits her knees in absolute defeat, in surrender. I see her look up towards the sky at a God she has cursed her entire life and ask for help. Ask, while she knows she has to do the work, if He exists, could He just point her in the direction her true self was. I watch her make a solemn vow to herself to do anything and everything to get through this. She will sleep fretfully that evening, much like countless others, but this night will be for different reasons. She knows she has to acknowledge and face everything that has happened in her life until this point. She knows she has to but is terrified to do so. She has never put blind faith into anything.

I watch as she gets up the following morning, watch her go about her regular routine. I see her complete her tasks inside and then head outside to do a few things. Her eyes become captivated by one of the stunning flowers in her garden. She feels the sun on her back in a warming, comforting sense. I watch as she looks up and admires the beautiful day. Not a cloud in the sky, and she feels thankful. Thankful for simply being outside in the wonderful world we live in. Thankful she confessed and owned her relapse. She feels her shoulders relax as she bends down to complete her tasks in the garden.

Suddenly, I watch a spark ignite from her entire being. I see her jolt in startled surprise and immediately go on the defense. There is a sensation going through her she has never felt before, and she doesn't have the slightest clue as to what it is. It is unknown, which equals dangerous or bad. In this moment, I am so grateful be able to see when she realizes what it is. I am able to witness the moment her walls drop to the ground—all of them. It is peace. Peace and freedom. She is battered. Bloody, bruised and burned, but she has done it. She has survived it. She has beaten the war she has been fighting her entire life. She is on top, in control, and aware. The realization of what it is again brings her to her knees, but this time in euphoria, thankfulness, and in knowing she isn't alone—she never has been. I see her bask in the knowledge of this and see the love and happiness that's been trapped inside her heart, behind all those walls, flow out of her in every direction, and she sees it. For the first time, she sees it—what she's capable of, all the good she can do, and all the wonderful aspects of her life. How lucky she is. How loved she is. She sees the light in front of her leading her to all of her hopes and dreams. She feels the safety of Him being with her always. She will go on to dedicate her life to helping others most people push aside or don't care about: the addicts and gang bangers, the drug dealers and convicted felons, the "dredges" of our society. Because she now sees people for whom they are, not what they seem. She sees the little boy or little girl in everyone hidden behind their own walls, wanting to be loved, held, and acknowledged, to be seen, to be heard, and to be cared about. She sees the underlying, untapped strength they have.

She realizes everything she battled—all the pain, suffering, and loneliness she went through—was necessary. It was necessary to become strong enough to have the ability to help others, to know the importance of taking responsibility for her own actions, to be able to shed the baggage that had her mind hostage. She sees her true purpose in life and will stop at nothing to achieve it. I watch as she walks, no, *runs* toward the light of faith, love, and peace, into open arms. Never to be alone again, she's home.

I'm no writer. At least, I never thought I was one. Hell, I don't even have my G.E.D. yet.

My name is Angelise Tomasino. I enjoy long walks on the beach, trees, SpaghettiOs, and reading. I am also an addict in recovery who's been through some shit. I survived it though, and wanted to find a way to help others see they are not alone—that being cracked or broken just means now there are ways for the light to shine both inward and outward.

I refuse to sit here with everything I've learned about life through my mistakes and let it go to waste. I refuse to worry about how people view addicts and how to make them understand our mindset anymore, so I am putting my heart and soul into this book to help fellow addicts, people who are lost and alone, *anyone* who needs someone to care. I do. It doesn't matter if we've never met. If you're reading this, just know I care, quite deeply, about you and your well-being.

There is no specific order to this. It's more like a jumbled pile of my thoughts, some quotes, and prayers that have helped me. It's my experiences and some things I've written. A few things will make you laugh and some will make you cry. It's random, disheveled, scatterbrained, and perfect in its imperfections, much like we are as humans. Fact is, life is messy and chaotic. Inside the chaos though, is where you can find the unending beauty.

Everything written in this has helped me in one way or another at one time. Sometimes, it is something as simple as a one-liner or stupid joke that helped me get through whatever I was going through at the moment. It always amazes me, the power of simplicity. I think many people, not just addicts, know what it's like to feel like there's twenty tabs open at the same time in your brain. Writing, I've discovered, is a very useful tool for me to be able to slow it down and decipher it all instead of feeling like I can't keep up or understand anything. There's something about being able to see your thoughts on paper that forces things into existence as well. It's harder to ignore my mistakes and wrongdoings, as well as my traumas, when they're staring me back in the face.

I hope this book brings you peace. I hope it makes you cry, and then I hope it makes you laugh. To quote one of my favorite movies, *Steel Magnolias*, "Laughter through tears is my favorite emotion." I hope it reassures you that you are not alone. I hope it brings you confidence and security. Most of all, I hope it brings you up. I love you all.

"Fear can hold you prisoner. Hope can set you free."
-The Shawshank Redemption-

There is an enormous difference between you knowing you made a mistake, and you acknowledging you made a mistake. There is also an enormous difference between you knowing you've been traumatized, and you accepting you've been traumatized. For me to be able to truly be happy and at peace, free from the proverbial chains that had held me down my entire life, I had to learn (the hard way, because I don't know how to do it any other way, apparently) how to face head-on all the terrible, ugly things I have done to people throughout my times during active addiction. I also had to learn to accept the bad shit I had been subjected to by others. These two things may seem simple enough, but it's much harder to stare at yourself in the mirror and face your demons and even harder to make them right. Until I did this, I wasn't able to successfully move on and let go of all the darkness and fear I was keeping harbored in my soul.

Acknowledging your mistakes goes hand in hand with accountability, responsibility, and honesty. Try to the best of your ability to apologize, atone for, and fix whatever it was that you did. The person may not forgive you for what you did, and that is their right. It's something I had to accept. I had no place deciding whether or not the person should forgive me. Either way, you will, at the very least, give whomever it was some closure to the matter. If you know in your heart that is the best you can do, so be it. In return, you'll be able to drop the load of that situation you had been carrying around. Man, it's crazy how good it feels. It's like losing a heavy, invisible brick that was on your chest. You become free from it.

Accepting your traumas goes hand in hand with bravery, self-love, and letting go. This realization gave me the courage to keep moving forward, to keep righting my wrongs, no matter the outcome. The initial act of confessing or admitting is always difficult, of course, but with each successful duty performed thus far, I have gained more and more of this inner strength I've never had before. I have done nothing but destroy and harm for almost twenty years. It feels amazing to be able to put something good, something honest, out there now.

Fuck fear. We're all scared on the inside in some way—of something/someone, all of us. It's part of life, experiencing fear, but don't let it hold you back. Stare it in the face and do the right thing. You take away its power by doing so, and that pushes you one step closer to a happy life—the one you deserve. Keep your hope alive, and your game face honest. Doing the right thing for the right reasons is a key to freedom, a key to peace, and you do deserve it, no matter what anyone else tells you.

I Shouldn't Be Allowed in Public Alone

Me at CVS: (Places seventeen cans of SpaghettiOs with meatballs on the counter.) Damn kids…all they'll eat is SpaghettiOs.

CASHIER: (Completely ignores me.)

ME: I have a lot of kids at my house, too. That's why I have to buy this many.

CASHIER: (Continues to ignore me, but I feel like she slowed down with scanning my items in a passive-aggressive, judgmental way.)

ME: In my day, if we didn't eat what was put in front of us, we didn't eat, period. Now they want SpaghettiOs three times a day."

CASHIER: (Doesn't even flinch. It's like I'm not even there.)

ME: Okay, *fine*, they're all for me.

I Shouldn't Be Allowed in Public Alone
Part 2

After I dropped my son off at school this morning and was walking toward the sidewalk, I noticed an individual waving her arms frantically in my peripheral. I made the mistake of making eye contact. (I may or may not have heard her yelling my name and didn't realize who it was until I saw her face.) So I suck it up, telling myself that this is fine (I'm fine. Are you fine? Because I'm fine.) and slap an awkward smile on my face as she approaches.

"Hey there, ha ha heh, you're a hard person to connect to in the morning. You always look kinda cranky!"

I become instantly aware my resting bitch face is, in fact, apparent. She just chose to ignore it, so now I hate her.

"Oh hey, ha, yeah, haha, not the first time I've heard that one, and probably not the last. Haha."

She then makes a little laugh, and proceeds to stare at me as if she's waiting for me to say something to her. I know for a fact nothing I have said could be derived as "Oh my God, *yes*, let's please continue this conversation," so I asked her, "Is there something I can do for you?"

To which she replies, "Nope, just wanted to say hello."

What? Why? She couldn't have just given me a little wave across the sea of other parents dropping off their crotch-goblins? Does she have any idea how much effort I put into looking unapproachable in the morning?

What follows after that is me making some strange throat noise and then turning and walking away. Hopefully, that is just as nerve-racking for her, so she knows better the next time she wants to have an intellectual conversation with me.

Thinking Is Difficult, That's Why Most People Judge

We live in a world where a little boy who needed a colostomy bag to survive committed suicide due to being bullied for having it. We live in a world where the homeless are stepped over, or on, by so many people instead of being helped and cared for, where people are murdered every day senselessly while people cheer for it to continue from the sidelines, where compassion and kindness are considered weak, while ego and pride are deemed important. How much money you have is how you're classified as successful or not in life.

Hate is encouraged by the media, and by our politicians. It has become the norm. Every day we read or hear stories of violence, racism, destruction and malice. It's everywhere we look, and everywhere we turn. It is thrust into our faces almost incessantly. We've accepted it, all of us, as-is, with the mindset that nothing will ever get better—that it's not our doing causing the issue at hand, so it's not our responsibility. To an extent, that is true. The act itself may not be your fault, but the way we react to it *is*. If someone hears a story of a banger who was shot and killed, and their thought is "Good, one less piece of shit in this world," I promise you that's not God talking. I get not everyone understands the street life mentality. That's good. I hope they will never have to wake up wondering if today will be the day they die or not, and they never have to live in a world where it's literally kill or be killed, where they wake up wondering if today will be the day they have to take someone else's life or not in self-defense. I hope they never understand the person who kills someone, but lives in a place where murder is glorified, so has to act hard or proud of the act they committed instead of displaying what it feels like to take a life, no matter if it was in self-defense or not. I hope they never have to live with the knowledge they killed someone, have their faces haunt their dreams at night, and being unable to talk to anyone about the anguish and despair pumping through their veins while pieces of their humanity chip away.

We're living in a generation suffering through an enormous opioid epidemic, and so many, many people do nothing but look down on and judge us addicts. They don't understand how someone can choose to take a pill or shove a needle in their arm continuously, many times at the expense of losing their families, prostituting, doing time, or winding up on the streets. No one is asking you to, or expects you to understand. To those who don't, just please, be grateful you've never felt a need so intense to numb away pain you willingly sell your soul to the devil to do so, that you haven't experienced lives full of rape, blood, and abuse in its most horrid forms, of being hated by your own parents, or abandoned by them, of dreading hearing something as simple as a door opening because it meant more of your innocence was about to be taken from you, of having a hand on your throat as you're raped while the sick fuck tells you he'll do the same to your sisters while you watch if you ever say anything to anyone. I am *so thankful*, you will never comprehend any of this, but please, please, stop judging what you don't know, and looking down on others whose journeys you have not experienced or lived. Trauma changes people, most of the time from the inside out.

If you see a person asking for money, don't look at him in disgust and refuse. Give him what you can spare. Sure, they may buy drugs or booze with it. You also may be the only reason they are able to eat that day. What they inevitably do with the money is their choice, but whether or not you do the right thing for the right reasons is on you.

It's overwhelming sometimes, all the sadness, anger, hate, and death, hence me writing this. I was not a good person for a very long time, full of animosity and selfish tendencies. It took me hitting my absolute rock bottom to see what I had become. It also showed me how far to climb though. We can't have the light without the dark, but it's your choice which one you live your life for.

I Am She

I am she, and she is me.
I am you, and you're me, too.
Him and her, her and he.
She is him, and he is she.

No more blood spilled, no more divide.
Just us together, side by side.
We're all brothers and sisters,
This is what I see.
While staring at the faces of humanity.

Not one good thing has ever stemmed,
In the name of destroying others.
Malice, hate, disgust and mistrust,
Do nothing but crush and abolish.

There's so much beauty in this world,
If we just turn around and face it.
But instead we choose turning our backs on each other,
And do nothing but continue to break it.

If we all helped one person every day,
Our world would change overnight.
Into a place filled with joy, gratitude and love,
Dark days no longer in sight.

You never know the battles others are fighting,
So try not to be angry or mean.
Instead try kindness and understanding,
Many have faced Hells you've never seen.

I will do my best to leave this world
A better, happier place.
No matter the trials, struggles and tribulations,
That I undoubtedly will face.

I wish I could give away freely,
All the love and peace in my heart.
Fill us all with compassion and trust,
To bring us closer instead of apart.

I hope I live to see the day,
That we all join hands and see,
Just how much better our lives can be,
If we embrace diversity.

-A.M.T.-

*Are oranges named oranges because they're orange,
or is orange called orange because oranges are orange?*

In the process of growing into who I truly am, I have acquired the ability to not respond so negatively to ignorance, understanding now a person's behavior toward someone or something always says more about the person themselves, rather than whomever or whatever their ignorance is directed toward. I've been rude to others, so I know rudeness much of the time stems from a place of inner pain. I've judged others, so I know placing judgement upon others is a result of my own fears or shortcomings, but as of late, I have seen a lot of hate and evil and it's getting to me, so I thought I would write this to hopefully bring forth another perspective in regards to all the murders taking place in Chicago.

Summer 2018, I began an anti-senseless violence movement called #come-findme. One of the things I do is go and secure declarations (a declaration is something I make for people murdered. It has their name, age and cause of death on it, as well as a promise from me stating their life will not be forgotten, nor will their death be in vain. I look up the area where someone was killed, go there, and tape their declaration to the nearest light or utility pole). The other day I headed to the city to secure four declarations, but was only able to complete two of them. The two I hung were both for fifteen-year-old boys, shot and killed within two days of each other—two babies, murdered in the streets. Yes, babies. Do you know what I see out there? What I feel? I see these people with guns, not at the age they are presently, but at whatever age they were when their brain got fucked for the first time from whatever trauma they went through. They saw a loved one get shot and killed in front of them. They were raped by a family member. They saw their mom OD in front of them. They were beat bloody by their father. They were abandoned by their parents. They were molested in the system. They were forced to prostitute to provide money for their parent's drug habits. Whatever atrocity flipped their mind at whatever age it happened. I don't see a couple young punks pointing guns at each other from opposing gangs. I see a five-year-old kid who saw his uncle's head explode in front of him from taking a bullet, pointing a gun at a seven-year-old kid who got the shit kicked out of him by his father while his mom nodded off on dope in the bedroom. I don't see a drug addict. I see a nine-year-old girl who is raped by her stepfather and hated by her actual father, so she turns to drugs to stop a pain that tears her soul into pieces. I don't see a shit head banger. I see a ten-year-old boy who grew up around nothing but blood in the streets from a very young age who knows nothing else—a ten-year-old who is told repeatedly by society he will never grow up to amount to anything and believes it.

Do I condone or support the violence and killings and lifestyle of the streets? No way. Am I defending the actions of murderers, gang bangers, or drug dealers? Fuck no. What they are doing is wrong on every level. It sickens me the amount of lives we're losing daily to drugs, the streets, and hate, but I understand the street mindset, as it is much like the addict's mindset. The next time you hear of someone being killed by gangs, try and picture the victim—or suspect, for that matter—as a child. Picture two small eight-year-olds pointing guns at each other—two kids who are terrified, *petrified* on the inside of having to pull the trigger on the other, crying hysterically, but have to maintain a tough front and act like they're not scared in front of the other kids. See the aftermath, of a five-year-old (inside) who just killed another five-year-old (inside). Feel the shock he feels of it actually happening, of him actually pulling the trigger. Feel how everything slows down like in a bad dream and the jolt that brings you back to the reality he just shot and killed someone. Picture a nine-year-old girl OD-ing on a park bench. Can you still be as objective when it's children in place of adults?

This shit isn't funny. It isn't a game. People are dying, *kids* are dying, and there are people who laugh or make jokes about it. I wonder if we all saw people as they truly are, if we could all feel what others are feeling and see what they see, if it would help things. I have done horrible, unspeakable things throughout my lifetime. I have hurt or betrayed almost every person that is in my life in some way. I've had guns pointed at me, had guns shoved to the back of my throat. I've been hurt and ripped open, shot, and stabbed. Raped, on drugs and left for dead. In prison and on the streets. On my knees giving head to get money to support my habit, and on my knees thanking God and the universe in gratitude for being alive. I've been to every level of Hell you can imagine plus a few more I created myself. My point being, our pasts do not have to define us. In fact, the only time that will happen is if you allow it to. Taking that first step toward the courage to face and deal with your past is where the healing begins almost instantly, and that's what others need to see— that there is another way, that life is beautiful and scary and magical and terrifying and amazing, that with hard work, integrity, honesty and perseverance, people *can* change, *can* better themselves. They need support and encouragement. They need to be accepted and cared about. This is how we change the world for the better, by coming together as brothers and sisters, extending helping, loving hands. It starts within each and every one of us.

•　　•　　•

FUCK. WALMART. That is all.

•　　•　　•

I had to take a quick walk to the CVS by my house to get a few things a little bit ago. I was enjoying the day, the sunshine on my face, and then BAM a fucking squirrel fell or slipped or some shit, landed on my shoulder, and scampered down my leg. It had been awhile since I shit myself, and the octave I reached while screaming was quite impressive if I do say so myself. I am also a black belt in karate now, if anyone would like lessons. My classes include having various forms of wildlife thrown at you while you use your panic and sheer terror to get them off, as well as the art of screaming from your soul.

> "Go and love someone exactly as they are. And then watch how quickly they transform into the greatest, truest version of themselves. When one feels seen and appreciated in their own essence, one is instantly empowered."
>
> -Wes Angelozzi-

So much truth and wisdom in this simple concept. We all desire and wish to be loved for who we truly are, not who we feel everyone else needs or wants us to be.

•   •   •

I can't explain why I made so many mistakes, why I repeated them knowing I was digging a hole that was getting deeper and deeper to climb out of. All I know is that I did. There's no way I could ever explain fully explain it or excuse it, but I own it. No one had a gun to my head forcing me to remain an addict. I may have been influenced, manipulated, or in pain by the hand or actions of myself or someone else, but in the end I said yes each and every time I used. Therefore, rather than try and make excuses or explain, I choose to be accountable.

Why is holding myself accountable important? Because accountability takes me from having a victim's mentality to having a victor's mentality. It puts me in the driver's seat, and gives me full control of my next move. The victim's mentality will take you down quicker than a toddler running full speed toward your kneecaps. I know it hurts, I know it rips you open, the things you've been through, but by allowing your past to dictate your future, they win. Rise up. There is a strength gained with each battle won, with each trauma faced. You become a survivor, not a victim. You *survived* those traumas. There are people out there who are not as fortunate. Don't let them win. You can overcome and move past anything you put your mind to, I promise you this. I believe in you.

• • •

"There is only one perpetrator of evil, and that is the human unconsciousness. If you were truly conscious of what your possible ill spirited actions does to another human being, to yourself and the collective unconscious, you would not do it. So those who act with toxicity in any manner, we have to understand that it is almost as if they are asleep. If they truly 'got' what they were doing they wouldn't have done it. You know this to be true."

-Eckhart Tolle-

• • •

Own It

"Own the fact that you are different. Own that you are a deep feeler and thinker. Own that you're tuned into a different frequency. Own the fact that you sense things others don't. Own the fact that you want to talk about angels, energy, miracles and spirituality. Own that you're done having meaningless conversations. Own that you're done holding yourself back. Own that you crave freedom to feel the now. It's ok if your family doesn't get you. It's ok if your friends don't join you. It's ok if the world judges you. It's ok that you want to dance barefoot upon the earth and endlessly gaze at the stars. It's ok that you cry over sunsets and chase moonbeams. It's wonderful, in fact. It's beautiful. You have come a long way to be who you are. So own it. Own all of it. Love all of you. The world needs you to be exactly as you are. You hold the balance in this crazy world.

-Eryka Stanton-

•   •   •

Me: *walks past nice bush*
Brain: Take some leaves.
Me: Why?
Brain: You gotta.

• • •

"Until you heal the wounds of your past, you are going to bleed. You can bandage the bleeding with food, with alcohol, with drugs, with work, with sex; But eventually it will all ooze through and stain your life. You must find the strength to open the wounds, stick your hands inside, pull out the core of the pain that is holding you in your past, the memories, and make peace with them."

-Iyanla Vanzant-

• • •

Someone asked me the other day if I'm scared of getting killed doing what I do with #comefindme. No, I'm not. The dangers surrounding what I'm trying to accomplish are known to me. I am at peace inside, and I know what's awaiting me, but what does scare me is someone killing me and then having to live with that the rest of their life, or having someone kill me who has already taken a life before me, thus becoming another nail in the sealed fate of the individual. Those notions terrify me, and have been the source of quite a few sleepless nights.... I don't want to be the reason anyone's humanity is defeated by their demons. I pray for the one wielding the gun just as much as the one who's on the receiving end of it.

• • •

Apparently, you can't use "beefstew" as a password. It's not stroganoff.

· · ·

Brain cell #1: Say, "Have a nice day."

Brain cell #2: No, no, say, "Have a good one."

My mouth: Haven gice done.

· · ·

God,

Grant me the serenity to accept the things that I cannot change, the courage to change the things that I can, and the wisdom to know the difference.

This simple yet powerful prayer saved my life on more than one occasion, even when I showed God every ugly corner I had.

· · ·

January 10th, 2019

"Some people appear in your life when you need them the most."

Last night I was out in Englewood, Chicago securing declarations, arriving at my first location at around 7:00 P.M. Per my usual routine, I went to the spot where an individual was killed, found the nearest light pole, parked my car, and threw on the hazards. As I was getting ready to exit my car, I saw someone out of the corner of my eye on my right side approaching me quickly. It is dark most nights when I am out, so I am always cautious and aware of my surroundings, as to be prepared for an altercation of any sorts if the situation presents itself. I saw it was a woman, and her stance wasn't menacing in any way, so I got out to go around the other side of the car to speak with her. You know what she wanted? To make sure that I was okay.

In her exact words, "I saw red hair, a white face, and your car was pulled over, I thought something was wrong." We talked for a bit while smoking a cigarette. I told her briefly about my friend, Adam Furtick, who was murdered senselessly a little over a year ago and some of the details as to why I was out doing what I was doing. She proceeded to tell me about her baby brother who was killed in 2006. He was a child at the time, eight-years-old, I think she said. The murderer was never caught. She told me I was crazy to be out there at night by myself. I assured her I was okay. Then she showed me her coat sleeve. Inside it, cupped in her palm, was an ice pick. She had been robbed, beaten, and raped out on those streets before, had witnessed a lot of hate and pain first hand, and she wasn't letting anyone get near her ever again without being able to protect herself. Every time she left the house, she stuck the pick in her sleeve. That was her reality and part of a daily routine in her life.

Not wanting to make her uncomfortable, I gave her my sincerest apologies about her current situation without it coming across as pity, said goodbye, and watched her continue down the street. I secured the declaration, got back into my car, and allowed myself to free the feelings from my chest about what this wonderful, friendly, caring lady had just confided in me. Waves of sadness and anger and downright heartbreak washed over me. At first I couldn't cry. Everything I was feeling was too intense, but as I processed the information given to me tears fell freely down my cheeks.

This lady amazed me. She was, in my opinion, who more people should look up to: compassionate and caring enough to check on a virtual stranger in an area frequent with crime, honorable enough to look me in the eye and stand proudly while speaking with me, regardless of the context of the words, smart enough to be prepared for any trouble but not start it or go looking for it even after having been personally affected by it on more than one occasion, and hopeful enough to believe the streets of Chicago can be changed.

I don't think meeting this woman was a mistake. As of late, I've been having trouble thinking of new ways to spread the message of #comefindme. I've felt like I haven't been doing enough and have had mounting guilt because of it.

Speaking with her for the ten minutes I did reaffirmed my faith in what I'm doing and brought back my confidence as to whether or not I will succeed. She gave me renewed strength and spirit, and in return I was able to give her some peace, some knowledge there is someone actively trying to put an end to the nightmare that has become hers, and so many other's lives. She left feeling more at ease, I left feeling lighter, and we both left better than we were previously. I hope I am lucky enough to come across her again at some point. She was an angel on earth to me last night at a time I most definitely needed it.

The lifestyle of this woman and thousands of others isn't in a foreign country. It isn't even across the country, or in a neighboring state. It's in Chicago, twenty-five minutes from where I live. It's happening now as we speak and breathe, and we can all help change this stigma simply by having compassion and respect for others. You can't help everyone, but we can all help one person. So choose kindness. Every time you're a judgmental person, we take a step backward instead of forward in humanity.

• • •

I'm reading a book called *The Art of Happiness* based on the ideals and beliefs of the Dalai Lama. There's something I read that resonated with me, and I wanted to share it with you all. It's a very interesting perspective, and I think there's a lot of truth to it.

He was speaking on individuals who consider themselves independent with the mindset they don't need anyone. They're perfectly fine on their own, which is typically the complete opposite for the basis of humans. We are not solitary beings by nature from either an emotional or logical standpoint.

Fact is, especially in the world nowadays, we *all* need people—all kinds from all backgrounds. The clothes on your back were made by other people. The machines used to help make the clothes on your back were made by people. The car you drive was built by someone else as well as the parts and machines and tools used to build the car. The cement you walk on was poured by someone else. Your money was made by other humans. The food you buy to eat or cook was grown, produced, or butchered by humans. The building in which you work in or live in, were made by humans. The water supply in your home is made possible because of other human beings, as well as your heat and air conditioning.

Literally almost everything in your life you use/own/eat/drink is made possible because of others. I know that I, personally, would have an extremely hard time if everything in my life I didn't make or grow myself were taken from me. We all need someone.

This notion humbled me and made me appreciate humanity in a way I didn't previously. Each one of us is blessed with our own unique talents, strengths, and gifts. I would not be where I am today without the assistance of thousands of others, and for that, I will always be eternally grateful. I only wish I understood sooner how important it is to accept others in my life graciously.

•   •   •

"We were all humans,
Until race disconnected us,
Religion separated us,
Politics divided us,
And wealth classified us."

Not certain who said this, but it's dead on balls accurate.

•   •   •

Bad puns. They're how eye roll.

•   •   •

People need to understand the second you choose to belittle, look down on, or judge someone is the same second you prove you are worse than they are. We are all the same imperfect creatures seeking love and understanding. Be kind.

• • •

My battle with addiction expands over the course of many years. In my younger days, there was a vast array of different drugs in my life, not one specific one, but pain pills…man. I fell in love hard and fast, and it would be a long time before I would willingly break free from its grasp.

Over the years I have been on many different medications from being diagnosed with PTSD, extreme anxiety, and depression. I'd be lying if I said they never helped me at any point because they have, but much like some of my previous coping mechanisms, although they had served their purpose in times of darkness, they were now causing me more problems than solutions. I hated being dependent on something to make me feel normal. Wasn't that a large basis of my addiction in the first place? Having to take pills to be happy?

Not to mention feeling like a robot at times. Sure, they assisted in making the lows feel not so low, but I started to realize I wasn't really feeling too much of anything, really. Something bad would happen, and I would be wondering why I wasn't more upset. Or at the other end of the spectrum, something good would happen, and I wouldn't understand why I wasn't more excited or happy. My sex drive was greatly diminished. For me, it was like living life in a plastic bubble. While the bubble helped eliminate anything negative from entering, it was also keeping out the positive as well. I began to speculate on that notion. Was I willing to sacrifice really feeling any joy, desire, or happiness for the sake of assistance in maintaining my negative feelings? Was it worth it to me?

Ultimately, it was not. My doctors were not pleased when I told them I didn't want to be on their medications anymore. They strongly advised against it until they realized I was going to do it no matter what they said, and then they tried to get me to go through a weaning off process. When I asked why that was necessary, they said stopping them abruptly would send me into withdrawal and wasn't good for me. My brain needed time to adjust to slowly having the medicine leaving my system.

That was the kicker for me. So they were telling me, an addict, who was addicted to pain pills (initially from me being prescribed them for too long from a doctor), the medicine they had me on was going to make me sick if I stopped taking it too quickly? You mean…like opioids? I remember the little laugh I gave when told that. What I told them was I survived the withdrawal process from pain pills. I would do the same from not taking the other man-made substances.

You can imagine how thrilled they were when I told them I would be smoking weed instead of taking anymore man-made substances to help me cope with anxiety, etc. I have smoked weed on and off for most of my life. I have never gotten sick from not taking it. The worst side effect I have ever personally experienced from weed is an uncanny love affair with Cheez Whiz (or snake cheese, as my daughter calls it). I sleep great. I have gained weight, finally, which is something I struggled with for years. I smile naturally, and am in a good mood most of the time. I have a ton more patience and energy to do things. I enjoy living even in the smallest moments.

There are quite a few people who feel since I am a pot smoker (*and* a mom, gasp!), I am not truly sober, and everyone is, of course, entitled to their own opinion. I just know in my case smoking weed has given me such a wonderful, real quality of life, one I've never experienced before. For me, it works. There are days that go by where I don't feel the desire to smoke at all, so I don't. And guess what? No withdrawal. I am not a slave to marijuana like I was with other things. Nope, not a slave, just an admirer, and I am eternally grateful for its existence. Have a migraine? Go take a hot bath and smoke a bowl. Can't sleep? Go pack my hitter box and take a step outside onto my deck. Nausea? Have the flu? Fibromyalsia acting up? Kids driving you nuts? Want to kill your husband? Here I come, water bong.

There are days in my past where those instances would've caused me to swallow a handful of pills, and for the simple fact that is no longer my life I feel blessed. I feel free. I am completely off of all medications for the first time in years, and I feel as if I was watching my life through regular TV until this point, and now I see it in HD. Weed has given me quality back instead of just living for quantity, and I will be a pot smoker till the day I die…and then I will come back and haunt you all, stoned as shit, leaving a trail of empty Spaghet-tiOs cans in my wake.

• • •

"For what it's worth; it's never too late or, in my case, too early to be whoever you want to be. There's no time limit, stop whenever you want. You can change or stay the same, there are no rules to this thing. We can make the best or the worst of it. I hope you make the best of it. And I hope you see things that startle you. I hope you feel things you never felt before. I hope you meet people with a different point of view. I hope you live a life you're proud of. If you find that you're not, I hope you have the courage to start all over again."

-F. Scott Fitzgerald-

• • •

My grandma called me fat today.

Now I know this may seem like a cruel thing for her to say. Let me assure you there was no malice in her words. You see, when I was in my active addiction, my average weight was anywhere between 100–110 lbs. I wouldn't eat most days, not wanting to "ruin" my high, and I drank a lot of soda. My height has been 5'7" for as long as I can remember, and I've always had a lot of muscle mass from playing sports and boxing and whatnot. Back in my late junior high and early high school days, I was a solid 140lbs, built like a brick shit house, able to bench 130lbs. without breaking a sweat.

Once I was heavy into using, I was retaining my muscle mass from working an insane amount of hours every week, but ended up losing a lot of my fat mass from barely eating anything for years. I looked like a super-fit string bean. Sexy, huh? I hated the way I looked. Looking in a mirror was a sure-fire way to instantly bring me down at any given point. You could see the bones protruding out of my shoulder blades, my hips, everywhere. It sickened me. Ironically enough, the depression I suffered due to my appearance was an aiding factor in my ongoing addiction. Crazy, isn't it? I hated the way I looked, so I took pills to numb my disgust, but it was taking the pills that were causing me to look and feel the way I was. Yet at the time, God Himself couldn't convince me to stop taking them, and around and around I went for a very long time.

As of almost a year ago, I had a goal weight of 150lbs. I wanted to reach. I am proud to say I have now surpassed my goal and am currently 157lbs. It's the biggest I've ever been, and I've never felt better. I have times where I feel self-conscious about how I look, but overall I am so happy with myself in a physical sense.

Ahhhh, my grandma. Some ways I would use to describe this iconic woman are tough with a rough exterior and a mouth that would make a truck driver blush. She grew up in difficult times and has worked hard her entire life. At ninety years old, she can undoubtedly still kick my ass. Getting a hug from her means a few solid thumps on your back that leave bruises. No nonsense. No bullshit. She's called me a motherfucker more times than I can count, and I couldn't love her more if I tried.

For this is the woman who, when she called me fat, had pride and love in her eyes. She did so at the sight of her now healthy granddaughter. She saw my curves, my internal glow, and she was proud. Her exact words to me were, "Have you seen the size of your ass?" after I called her out on commenting on my weight, and it couldn't have made me feel better if she had told me I looked beautiful. I saw the tears she was holding back and heard the catch in her throat when she said it. I have done a lot to let my grandma down over the years, but she has forgiven me for everything, and I still get the same "mean" treatment as the rest of the grandkids. No, she isn't the quintessential picture of what a grandma is "supposed" to be, but I like mine better. Per every curse word thrown in our direction, there was a trip to the goodie drawer in her kitchen. She's the one who taught me how to be strong and capable. She was the grandma who would have Easter egg hunts and sleepovers for all of us cousins, whose living room is still decorated in the most beautiful ways during the Christmas season. Who bakes dozens of cookies for the holidays and passes them out to all of her loved ones. She's the woman who, when she was told she had breast cancer, told the doctor to "cut the fucking thing off, and take the other one with you if you want." She's the one I could always talk to when I was younger who never turned her back on me. I learned my love of gardening through watching her take care of her own. She taught me to be responsible, to work hard, and to not take shit from anyone.

My gram was a sheriff on 26th and California at the C.C.D.O.C. (Cook County Department of Corrections) for many years, retiring only when she was diagnosed with breast cancer. I'll never forget the time when I was younger and we went to the mall for something. As we were attempting to leave the parking garage, she wound up accidently turning down the wrong way, and we were left going head-to-head with another car. The guy in the other car instantly started being a dick. I get it, she was going the wrong way, but the way he was acting was ridiculous. To my gram's credit, she handled it pretty well…at first. She knew it was her fault and wasn't trying to say otherwise. He proceeded to get shittier and shittier, but she kept her cool. Until, that is, he decided it would be a smart idea to exit his vehicle and approach hers with the intent of berating her face-to-face. As soon as he started getting out of his car, her bitch switch flipped. I have never seen someone switch a car into the park position and hop out of it as quick as she did.

Before he knew what was happening, she was sauntering her way over to him, asking him, "What are you going to do, huh, motherfucker?"

That's when he told her he was going to get the law involved. Her counter to that? To grab her sheriff's badge out of her purse, shove it in his face and scream, "I am the law! Now do I have to beat your ass, or are we done here?"

I am crying from laughing, typing this story out. I have no doubt who would've won that fight. I'll leave it at that.

This past November (2018), my ninety-year-old grandma took a spill in her house. For the next two weeks, despite being uncomfortable or in pain from the fall, she went about her everyday life working at Target (yep, still worked at ninety, something to keep her busy), taking care of her house, cooking. She hosted Thanksgiving at her home, even. Well, the morning after Thanksgiving, she couldn't get out of bed. That fall she took two weeks previous had broken her hip, and she had no idea.

Breaking a hip isn't an easy recovery for anyone, let alone a ninety-year-old woman, but the old battleaxe wasn't giving up without a fight, and in the weeks to follow she would go on to amaze not only her loved ones but the doctors, nurses, and physical therapists in charge of her health and recovery. In just a couple short months, she was able to go back to her house. She has a fancy wheelchair she rides around in now, and you can see the peace and happiness in her face from being home as opposed to a hospital or rehab facility. Her blood, sweat, and tears are laced throughout that house—her memories, her good times, and bad—the home in which she lived with her late husband, my gramps, the home in which he passed away in. It's her safe place, and she is thriving now that she's back in it.

She told me on one of the visits I made to see her with my kiddos while she was in the rehab center, "Angelise, I'm gonna walk the fuck out of here, you just wait and see."

Never did I doubt this incredible, amazing woman would do just that, and she did with pride. She did it with grace. She did it with integrity. She did it with all the aspects of who she was, with all she had been through and survived up until now. It was one of the most precious moments of my life, seeing her return home after single-handedly defeating not only the war, but also every battle along the way leading up to it throughout this experience in her life. I can only hope to be half the woman that she is, if I am fortunate enough to live that long. I love you, Gram.

•　　•　　•

Anyone need an ark? I Noah guy.

•　　•　　•

"The one who plants trees, knowing that he will never sit in their shade, has at least started to understand the meaning of life."
-Rabindranath Tagore-

•　　•　　•

"If you don't heal what hurt you, you'll bleed on people who didn't cut you."
-Unknown-

Absolutely.

• • •

My daughter Annabel, the precious delicate angel:

> "DaDdY dOeS tHe ToOtHpAsTe BeTtER. YOuRs iSn'T
> As SmOoTh As dAdDy'S."

Then she turned around with her hands on her hips and walked away.

Me to her back:

> *giving her the finger*
> "Okay great, thanks for stopping by."

• • •

Ocotber 2016, this was when I had my suicide planned.

The details as to why aren't important. At the time, I was going through a lot and suffering in silence because I refused to talk to or let anyone in to help me. Although sober from pain pills, I still lived my life revolved around my addict's mentality, and it had gotten me to the point where I no longer saw a light at the end of the proverbial tunnel. I was done. My kids, fiancée, family, and friends, I was convinced were better off without me. So, my upcoming hysterectomy I had scheduled due to being diagnosed with cervical cancer gave me the perfect opportunity to end it all. It was there in the hospital I would take my own life.

I would end up not going through with it, not because I wouldn't have, but because my plans were thwarted (thankfully) by my secrets coming to light. Although very upset, angry, and disappointed in me, my loved ones who were aware of the circumstances at the time rallied around me and refused to give up on me even though I deserved for them to do so. It would be awhile before I would really become "okay" in my mind and heart, but it was the first time I had hope that maybe, just maybe, I wasn't a worthless piece of shit and deserved love and happiness.

The other day, a little boy in seventh grade within my son's school district brought a gun to school, went into the bathroom, and shot himself. From the moment I heard about it, there's been a searing pain in my chest. It's not the first baby we've lost to suicide, not even close, and it seems like these kids are getting younger and younger.

I haven't been able to get this out of my head, for multiple reasons. I'm not certain of the details surrounding this poor kid's death, nor do I care to speculate the whys. The bottom line is a child's life is over at his own hand due to whatever turmoil was eating at him. In seventh grade before his life even had the chance to start it was over, and that fact shatters me.

I'm not a doctor, a psychiatrist or a therapist. I don't know the ins and outs of the human brain, generally speaking, but I know what I've survived, where I've been, and where I am now. I know pain and trauma change you. I know this world is filled with people who feel as if they have no one. That is a feeling etched into my soul for the majority of my life, but most importantly I know it gets better. In my case it took a lot of hard work, honesty, and letting go. I had to forgive as well as own my mistakes and the aftermath of my choices.

Here's what kills me about situations like these though. I'm thirty-four years old, a grown woman. Defeating my demons was by far the hardest thing I have ever had to do. This long journey of mine has almost killed me a few times, and I'm an adult. This child, this twelve year boy, took his own life before ever knowing it wouldn't feel the way he was feeling now forever.

Our babies need us. They need us so much. They need our attention. They need our love, dedication, compassion, and understanding. They need kindness. They need to feel safe. They need to know they're not alone. They need to know we care about them and their well-being. They deserve a chance to grow up happily. They deserve to make mistakes without fear, to have us lead them to be good-hearted people. They deserve to have a safe place to live where their innocence is protected instead of shattered. They deserve all this and more. Sometimes those who need love the most ask for it in the most un-loving ways, so don't turn your back on anyone, but children especially. Hurt children, much of the time, grow up to be adults who hurt people because it's all they know.

•　　•　　•

I am going to do my best to describe my outing yesterday for #comefindme, but I'm not certain if I know the words to depict just how amazing, heart-warming, and incredible it truly was.

Yesterday was a hard, sad day. Suffice to say, many of us were following the story on AJ, a little boy who went missing in Illinois, and while in the back of my mind I knew he was gone, my heart refused to listen and remained hope-ful he would be found alive. The police finding his body made me crumble to the ground. I felt his loss, his absence. It was a crushing development to say the least.

I knew I would be heading out to secure declarations last night and was trying very hard to prep myself for it. My soul was in turmoil as it was, and going to areas where people's lives were recently taken from them was only going to make it worse. The closer to Austin (a part of Chicago) I became, the worse it got. After I jumped off 290, I pulled over for a bit to gather myself. My fucking hands were killing me from gripping the steering wheel too tightly, I was having a hard time breathing, and my whole body was shaking uncon-trollably. I let the emotions go and just cried—ugly cried—for a bit. I prayed for peace to be able to do my duty with grace and integrity. I prayed for peace for AJ. I prayed for peace for the people of Chicago. I prayed for peace for people in general. When I felt more in control, I moved forward with com-pleting my tasks for the evening.

It was a beautiful evening weather-wise, so my pup and I were riding with the windows down. The streets were brimming with people walking around and laughing. There were people hanging out in front of their homes and storefronts. Kids were playing. Music was playing. It made me smile on more than one occasion, and it would be here, in Austin, the part of Chicago with the most homicides thus far this year, I would receive the deep, serene peace I was so desperately seeking.

The sounds were sounds of life, of joy, of contentment…of having fun, and being happy. A few people approached me while I was securing declarations, curious as to what I was doing. They pet and played with my dog, whom you have no choice but to love instantly. There were smiles shared, as well as mutual respect and gratefulness, and to top it off the sun set in the sky and left behind a magical display of colors that were so beautiful it left me in awe. It stunned me into appreciative silence. The pictures I captured of it don't do it justice at all.

It was while admiring this sunset I was hit with the realization AJ was now at peace. He wasn't in pain anymore. No, now he was happy, safe, secure, and—oh my God—loved. He is loved so deeply and is in His arms. He is at rest, free to do whatever it was that precious little boy loved doing the most, and he is smiling. He's okay, you guys, and so are the other victims of violence whose lives were taken that I was out for last night. Call me crazy, but I can't shake the knowledge AJ was welcomed by each and every one of them. He has a family now, one that will love and comfort him unconditionally. There is no hate, pain or fear where he is. He is safe and at peace in the arms of a Father who loves us all. He's free and shining brightly, a guardian angel over us all, joined hand-in-hand with all the other angels in Heaven.

R.I.P., AJ

• • •

Things I Never Thought I Would Say

(If someone can show me in the parenting handbook where it shows you how to properly handle these situations, I will give you $1,000,000.)

Let go of the dog's balls!

Your penis doesn't belong on the window. Put it back in your pants.

It doesn't belong on the window *sill* either

I wish someone would send *me* to my room

I'm sorry you can't take your nipples off, there's literally nothing I can do to help you with that.

What, *stop*! Stop jumping on your brother's head. It's not a trampoline!

Your sister *is not* a power ranger gone rogue, she's just an asshole sometimes. Why is she an asshole? Because half of her DNA is mine. Yes that means I'm an asshole too. I'm sorry me being an asshole made her an asshole who ended up being an asshole to you, but it also means *you're* half an asshole. Use your powers for good, not evil…unlike your sister.

She stuck three raisins up her nose…Yes, three…No, all in the same nostril.

• • •

The next time you touch me I'm coming after you. I'm coming after you, your loved ones, and your friends. I'll destroy them all, you hear me? You tell 'em I'm coming, and Hell's coming with me!

-Me to my shower curtain when is grazes my leg-

• • •

I had a huge breakthrough not too long ago, and the other day my therapist asked me how I was doing with everything. The following is how I describe not only my current mindset, but also my best attempt to describe how it used to be. My hope is it helps someone, even if it's only one person.

I've always had a special connection to trees. All kinds, all sizes, and shapes. Imagine standing in a field, and staring at a line of trees in front of you. There's a deep, dark forest behind that line, with trees growing thick among each other. A never-ending maze with seemingly no light able to shine through. Foreboding and ominous, nothing but branches intertwining and shadows. That is what my brain has always felt like to me. Getting through it safely is not something I ever deemed possible. There were no trails. How would I keep from getting lost? There was no sun, How would I see? And what the fuck was at the center of it all anyways?

So there I would sit on the proverbial sideline for many, many years. This knotted, impenetrable mass of trees was something I always knew I needed to get through, but fear held me back until the day I was done. I was done allowing myself to be a victim, done not holding myself accountable, done merely surviving instead of actually living.

I would go on to, for the first time in my life, take responsibility for my actions, and confess my relapse. From there I would find a therapist and start putting in serious work on myself not only in therapy, but on my own time daily as well, and through being honest, open, and fair to myself I began to see change almost immediately. It became apparent to me I spent much of my life trying to burn the fucking forest down, which in essence was what was killing me. No, I needed to spend time with each tree, nurture it, and make peace with it. I needed to accept them, all of them, as a part of myself. I needed to forgive others as well as myself.

Tree by tree, trauma by trauma, whether self-inflicted or otherwise I began to face my forest. I would separate it from the chaos within and plant it in its own individual place. I would be patient with myself and allow the emotions that had built up around the tree to flow freely, understanding the only way to rid myself of the pain was to go through it. After I felt "clean" from the trauma at hand, in my mind I would plant an orchid (my favorite flower) beneath the tree, with the intent of its roots reaching that particular tree, and the two essentially becoming one. Bringing light to the darkness, therefore restoring balance. See that's a big key to eternal happiness, I think. It's not about getting rid of the forest. Destroying it only destroys you. It destroys your soul, your humanity. We *need* the dark parts of our pasts. They're how we learn strength, honor, and integrity, by facing and making peace with them, by staring our demons in the eye, and learning how to tell them to fuck off without blinking. How is one to know, understand, and appreciate the light if they first don't come from the dark?

I was quite proud of myself for how well I was progressing. There was an inner strength laced in my blood I had never felt before, and I woke up grateful every day. Then the evening of my birthday, while watching *Ghost Adventures* and looking forward to multiple orgasms from Jay (sorry mom), my brain decided to unleash what would come to be the "beginning" of everything for me. By that, I mean the specific event that first initially twisted my mind up came into my consciousness, and turned my world upside down. This was March 11th 2019, and I am still recovering from this remembrance, breakthrough, whatever you want to call it.

But...*but*...me reaching the point of origin that would begin my slow descent into the seventh circle of Hell was such a blessing. Sure it hurts. Some days it's hard to breathe. I am still shocked by the connections it has to everything. Initially, the first few days preceding it especially, no, it did not feel like a blessing. It felt like drowning and being incessantly electrocuted at the same time. I was raw, open, and exposed, and it took patience (both with myself and the situation at hand), persistence, and being brave to get through the beginning part of what I would come to recognize as complete and total healing from what the darkness in me had created.

The beauty and clarity that has risen from dealing with this trauma has been one of the most precious moments in my life. Through dealing with my pain and anguish properly, which for me means with therapy, being open and honest and loving myself, all the trees in my forest are now in neat rows. They have their own space and are all connected to the same water source I found in the center of them (my soul). I can walk through them all, able to see and acknowledge each one individually with ease, without being shrouded in darkness or uncertainty. Each tree has brought beauty into my life, whether it was through a blessing or a lesson. I know that now. Not a single one has been removed or destroyed.

I still haven't visited every tree yet. I haven't placed an orchid on all of the dark ones to bring light to them, but I stood up to, faced, nurtured, and made peace with my biggest, most ominous one. There is an inner light in that tree that illuminates the path to all of the other ones with which I need to come to terms—which with I *will* come to terms. I have no fear left in me, none. I have embraced my forest, the whole thing, and you can find me dancing happily in the glorious fountain in the center of it.

I will never lie and say the way to inner peace is easy, or that it feels good all the time, but I will tell you from the bottom of my heart it's worth it, so worth it. It's okay to be scared at first. Shit, it's 100 percent normal to be scared, but you have to make the decision to not let fear be what propels you through your life. It's a 1,000lb. invisible weight on your chest that will prevent you from making any serious growth or change. Be scared, but keep moving, and watch how the fear just melts away. The only thing I'm scared of now is this article I read that said if spiders ever figure out they could, they have the ability to take over us all. Because I got me. I got me, and God and the Universe have me.

•   •   •

"Hard is not relative. Hard is just…hard. There is no 'harder.' There's just…hard. We need to stop ranking our hard against everyone else's hard to make us feel better or worse about our hard. And just commiserate on the fact that we all have hard.

At some point in our lives we all live in closets. And they may feel safe...at least safer than what lies on the other side of that door. But I'm here to tell you, no matter what your walls are made of, a closet is no place for a person to live."

-Ash Beckham-

This is such an enormous key to lasting peace. The minute we realize and accept we all experience the same feelings, in regards to what are deemed the highs, lows, and middle points of life, is the moment your whole world changes in ways you can't imagine. I haven't felt lonely since this realization, and coming from a woman who spent her entire life in her "closet," the gratitude I hold is unprecedented. I now see, acknowledge, and understand the importance of speaking openly and without fear because we all feel it all. By opening up about our lives to one another about our traumas, troubles, and anxieties we gain the ability to learn about each other, see things we don't see, hear things we haven't heard, all while being able to have genuine empathy for others because we understand the feelings others are feeling, and we now become aware others understand us as well. The *experiences* in life, be it positive or negative, are what make us unique and special, not the feelings attached to them.

Take a seven-year-old girl who saw her mom get shot and killed in front of her, and a ten-year-old boy who lost his mom to cancer. Both children have suffered trauma, a deep and painful one. Losing a parent is Hell, no matter the circumstances. Now the circumstances pertaining to the individual losses themselves may not be the same, but the sadness, grief, shock, anger, loss, and emptiness each child feels is the same. That's because these feelings are the natural reaction to things such as this. The events leading to the loss don't need to be the same; it's the loss itself that is. That's where empathy comes in to play and is what makes us all connected, whether we want to acknowledge it or not. This is also where you can find some peace knowing you're literally surrounded by people who know what loss feels like. None of us get through life without experiencing loss.

This basic principle applies to adults as well. Say a man loses his brother to a car accident and a mother loses her friend in an armed robbery. Again, the details involved in each event may be different, but the feeling of loss and heartache is identical. That is the common ground. This is where we are the same. Each person has the ability to empathize with another person's loss, and it is here through empathy and understanding we will be faced with the undeniable truth that we are not alone, and we never really were.

I know how difficult and terrifying the notion is to open up to people about your "closet." You know why it's terrifying? Being vulnerable isn't easy. It isn't easy to share your pain or to ask for help. That's why being vulnerable makes you strong—strong as fuck. We all crave and search for love and understanding, but it takes inner strength to not only do the work to get it, but to be open to receiving it as well. I don't know when or where being open, honest, and sensitive began being deemed as weaknesses, but I do know that sentiment is wrong on every level. I was a hard person who would rearrange your face for looking at me funny for most of my life. Now I openly accept the difficulty that comes with speaking my feelings freely. There is no freedom like inner freedom. The Devil himself can't pry my big, soft, sensitive heart out of my chest no matter how hard he tries because I am love. I accept love and I give love.

●　　●　　●

I must have a sign on my head that says, "Fuck with me, I make funny faces," or something.

I like to garden, always have. It brings me peace. I took a picture of the seedlings I had planted and posted it on Facebook and spoke of my excitement for this year's veggies and herbs. A few days later, I ran into one of the moms from my son's school at the store.

She said to me, "Looks like a nice garden you have this year!"

I smile and say, "Yep."

Then she says to me, "I didn't know you guys liked doing stuff like that."

I'm already irritated because I have my daughter holding my hand while going full dead weight, they're out of Cheez Whiz, and I'm trying to balance all the items in my right arm because I don't need no stinking cart (I always need the fucking cart, I just never take it). I have no idea what she means by "you guys" so I said, "You guys...?"

To which she replies, "Oh hahaha, you know, people in jail. I didn't know you like to garden."

I stare at her. She stares back at me. Then to help ease the discomfort I said, "Well, I got a pair of heavy duty gloves and a shovel upon entering the I Am A Felon club. Only seemed natural to learn how to use them for *other purposes*," and proceeded to stare at her with my eyes wide open.

Dumbass. Dumb to the ass.

•   •   •

"Our souls fell in love. Our egos broke us up."
                                             -Bridgett Devoue-

My Jay and I? We've been through some SHIT together. You name it, we have experienced it in one way or another. The things we've survived would tear apart most other couples, but through the chaos is where we grew together and became able to have the foundation we do now, so I thought I would write about what we've learned through our trials and errors. It took a lot of growing up to do, and a lot of owning up to and making peace within us.

In my experience, there are two reasons we react defensively to altercations: We feel shame or guilt from previous actions, or we feel shame and guilt from current actions. On the surface it may look and feel like anger within us, but anger is a blanket emotion that hides the truth many times. In fact, that's how I view it in my head. I see anger covering all of my other emotions I'm feeling, much like a big blanket, and it's hiding beneath that blanket of anger that will prevent you from ever making any real, lasting progress.

This is why making peace within yourself is so important. Until you do, it debilitates you in ways you don't see but will leak out onto others that you love. Guilt is a big cloud of ugly that will hold you back from being happy if you let it do so, and in order to properly release the guilt you are carrying, your effort to make it right needs to match your effort in whatever act it was you committed. Good people do bad things in relationships sometimes. It's that simple. We all fuck up. It's okay. What's not okay is continuing down the path of self-destruction that burns others in your presence.

You need to own it. You need to look at yourself in the eye and say *I fucked up*. Nevermind all the excuses as to why you did what you did. It doesn't matter. It doesn't matter if the other person hurt you first. It doesn't matter if they deserved it. Making decisions based on other people's actions is the quickest way to Hell, I promise you. It doesn't matter that you've got a fucked up past and you're jaded and scarred. *You* are responsible for your own internal healing, no one else. This world owes you nothing, and if you waste your time thinking it does, you have a long and lonely life ahead of you. Once you admit to yourself what you did was wrong and 100 percent own it, you automatically open a doorway to move forward. Here you will be at a crossroads, and you will have to make the decision to either go down the road toward healing or the one that will eventually take you right back to where you were.

Working on yourself and your issues is hard, man, especially at first. If it were an easy thing, cleansing your body and mind of all the darkness, everyone would do it. The mistakes you've made, I can guarantee you millions of others have. There's nothing unique about feeling shame or guilt, as we all do at points in our lives. The important thing is to learn from our mistakes and do whatever we need to do to correct the line of thinking that allowed us to commit whatever act it was in the first place. Find what works for you. For me it's therapy, reading, and writing. These three things have changed my life around in ways I never thought possible. The idea of me seeing a therapist seven years ago would've been laughable at best.

You know what one of our biggest issues has been our entire lives, Jay and I? Our egos. It was our egos that kept us in a state of a victim's mentality. It was our egos that made excuse after excuse for our bad decisions and behaviors, and it wasn't until we began to temper down our egos we found it possible to have peace. This isn't an art you can practice and perfect. You can only remain humble, and it's through humility you learn how to balance your ego with empathy, honesty, and compassion. It's not trying to get rid of your ego, it's balancing it and learning how to work with it. When you fuck up (and you will fuck up, you're a human being, we all do), own it. That's how you restore the balance there, but remember changed behavior is the best way to apologize. Anything less is manipulation. It's okay to make mistakes. It's not okay to make mistakes with no intention of doing the work necessary to fix yourself. That is the epitome of selfish.

Practice lives of honesty and integrity, and soon you won't have to practice it, it simply becomes second nature. You will welcome accountability because you see the peace you receive in return. Sometimes you can't fix what you broke, but you can bring closure to the person you wronged by taking full responsibility for your actions, and that is the best you can do; simply do the best you can.

•　　•　　•

I've spent a large portion of my life battling the disease of addiction. On June 16, 2019, I'll celebrate my first year clean, both from the drug itself and from the addict's mentality (it's May 10, 2019 as I write this). This anniversary is going to mean the world to me because I have *never* been free from the mentality of an addict. I relapsed last year right before what would've been four years clean, and I 100 percent believe it was because I never changed my thinking patterns.

I was putting all of my time and effort into all the wrong areas. I wasn't working on my issues or learning to love myself. Instead, I was living my life exactly the same with the exception of using, so I was also fighting the urges and cravings to use on top of everything else. I still hated myself and my past and refused to face them. My relapse was inevitable, and quite frankly, I'm surprised it took as long as it did to happen.

First and foremost, I had to face and accept my past. Nothing would be lasting for me until I did, and it took me relapsing to see that, so it ended up being a blessing in disguise. In hitting my rock bottom, I was able to see just how far I had to climb. Little by little, day by day, I began to gain strength, an internal strength that makes you feel as if you could move mountains. That's the only way I know how to describe it. This strength also ties into willpower. Your willpower, I have discovered, must be stronger than your emotions. Life sucks sometimes, and there's no avoiding it, but when you let the people, places, and things surrounding you dictate what your next move will be, you surrender your own happiness at the expense of others. No one can be truly happy living that way.

•   •   •

" I think that how you perceive life as a whole plays a role in your attitude about suffering. For instance, if your basic outlook is that suffering is negative and must be avoided at all costs and in some sense is a sign of failure, this will add a distinct psychological component of anxiety and intolerance when you encounter difficult circumstances, a feeling of being overwhelmed. On the other hand, if your basic outlook accepts that suffering is a natural part of your existence, this will undoubtedly make you more tolerant towards the adversities of life."

-Dalai Lama-

•   •   •

"Your shitty childhood isn't an excuse to be a shitty person. Your shitty luck with relationships isn't an excuse to be a shitty person. Your shitty experiences aren't an excuse to be a shitty person. We ALL have our own shit, and you can either let it define you, or you can grow from it."

-Unknown-

· · ·

"I think we all have to go through times of stress, confusion and complete frustration. Times of loneliness and desperation. I think it's in those moments, that you truly find yourself. For when you come out of it all; when you manage to find that strength in yourself to calm down and have faith that you can take on anything, is when you discover happiness. Just like when you fight with someone you love and you manage to work through it and it just makes your relationship that much better for not giving up in tough times.

So don't expect your life to never see a rainy day.

It's the hard times that make us realize what we are capable of, they are what make us realize what we really want in life. How we achieve our goals and dreams, and how we find forever with someone. I think that's what life is really about. Proving that you can stay strong through everything that's supposed to make you weak."

-Unknown author, on finding fulfillment-

· · ·

"People often hold the thought that if they forgive someone, they are doing the person they've been angry at a favor…not realizing that forgiveness is, first and foremost, a favor one does for oneself. Forgiveness is an act of self-interest. We do it so as not to let our judgments and anger bind us up in somebody else's ignorance, fears, problems. In some cases, we do it so we don't get lost in somebody else's nightmare. If, for example, you were physically abused by an alcoholic parent, you were most likely locked into years of misery. Forgiving that parent can't erase the past. However, it can lead you out of the nightmare that you were pulled into as a child, and it can help you to heal from the aftershock now. Forgiving can restore the personal power that you were robbed of.

Although our egos work to convince us that if we forgive we will be weakened, true forgiveness is actually what strengthens us. In a place that can be as dark and negative as prison, forgiveness looks like an unlikely tool for survival. But in fact, that is just what it is.

-Robin Casarjian, from the book "Houses of Healing, a Prisoner's Guide to Inner Power and Freedom-

• • •

May 12, 2019

Today was Mother's Day. I've been a mother on paper since my incredible son was born on October 11, 2012, but this was the first Mother's Day I felt worthy of being one.

This isn't easy for me to admit out loud, never mind putting it in a book for others to read, but up until my relapse I was a shit mom. It's not that I didn't love my babies, or I wouldn't go up against anyone in this world who tried to hurt them. They weren't neglected in any basic need and they had plenty of toys and books. The love I felt for them was unmatched, just like it is now. My heart? They owned, every inch, but my head….

My head was twisted up with my priorities ass-backwards. Fact is, my addiction had been number one in my life for a very long time. And even while being clean for nearly four years, I still had the same thinking patterns. I was miserable and angry and sad. My babies did not have 100 percent of their mommy. I was selfish. I was *wrong*.

I never, ever wanted to hurt my kids. I didn't wake up in the morning with the intent to be less than they deserved, but I wasn't choosing to wake up every day with the intent of working on my issues and me either.

When I say my relapse was a blessing I mean it in every sense of the word. It gave me a fresh start. I knew I didn't want to be the person I had been for much of my life any longer, and I was determined to pull my head out of my ass. This journey toward self-healing and discovery this past year has been incredible. Trying, for sure, but incredible. It's no easy feat, reaching into your soul to grab the source of your pain by its roots and rip it out, but it's a necessary struggle that will ultimately lead you out of the darkness.

You don't realize how very much so you are your own worst enemy until you start to do the work on yourself. Working through your pain, the darkness you carry in you, is the way towards the light. Do this, and lasting peace and freedom are *yours*.

Today I can say I am worthy of being my kids' mother. I can say with a smile on my face that learning to love me for who I truly am was the key to me being the best mommy I can be to my babies. My struggles have all been turned into blessings because without them, I wouldn't be as strong as I am now. Each and every trauma I went through and survived taught me a lesson, and I am so thankful for everything I have learned thus far.

• • •

It is an absolutely gorgeous day outside today, and I can't keep up with the tears that keep coming from how grateful I am to be alive and clean from opioids. I feel pure, on fire with passion, and so blessed. Never in a million years did I ever think I'd love my life the way I do, but here I am. I am a living testament that anything can be overcome with willpower, integrity, honesty, and hard work, and just know that I believe and have faith in you too.

• • •

Check Yourself

Sometimes you are the toxic person. Sometimes you are the mean, negative person you're looking to push away. Sometimes the problem is with you, and that doesn't make you less worthy. Keep on growing. Keep on checking yourself. Mistakes are opportunities. Look at them, own them, grow from them, and move on. Do better. Be better. You're human. It's okay.

-Unknown-

• • •

I yearn for a different world, one where people can agree to disagree respectfully, where people can love whomever they choose to love and have it be accepted as long as it's not hurting them or someone else. One in which I'm not afraid to let my son walk the one block to school by himself like he asks me to do, for fear of some monster kidnapping him. A world where there is no rape or sodomy. Where money isn't the root of all evil. Where all of our priests protect our kids instead of molesting them. One where cops are treated with dignity and respect and one where they all deserve it. Where people own their own mistakes, and accept while we are free to make our own choices, we are not free of the consequences of our actions. Where addiction of any kind is nonexistent. A world where our children grow up happily with their families, where we teach the importance of hard work, integrity, loyalty, and honesty. A world in which we are not ashamed of God, in whatever form He is to each of us. A world where the cures for fatal diseases aren't buried beneath greed but instead administered to those who need it without hesitation to help save their lives. One in which *no* child is beaten, abandoned, hurt, or killed. One where teachers make more money than professional athletes. A world with bookstores on every corner instead of McDonalds. Where you're not judged by the color of your skin, by the mistakes you make, or the pasts you carry, but instead are met with compassion, kindness, and the willingness to be understanding. One where people pay attention to common sense and their consciences. Where our brave police officers and vets aren't committing suicide. Where our babies aren't committing suicide. Where our brothers, sisters, mothers, fathers, sons, daughters aren't committing suicide. A world where our government has we the people's best interests at heart. One where we look out for each other instead of our own asses. Where all of our food and water is healthy and not full of chemicals, and our air is clean. A world where showing love isn't viewed as a weakness, but instead recognized as strength. One in which we see each other exactly how we truly are inside, and we cherish each and every human being as a gift, as a friend, as a person. Where there is no hate, racism, or divide.

A shark in a fish tank will grow eight inches, but a shark in the ocean will grow eight feet or more. The shark will never outgrow its environment, and the same is true about people. Sometimes we're around small-minded people, so we don't grow. Change your mindset and just watch how you grow.

•   •   •

One of the greatest things about God is that He'll bring you out of the situations you got yourself into and not hold it against you. He will not heal your traumas for you. That is up to each and every one of us, but best believe He is right by your side, cheering you on. He has *never* given up on me, even when

I was cursing Him and His very existence. With all our downfalls, mistakes, and weaknesses He thinks the world of us. This knowledge brings me so much happiness because we all had a purpose before others had an opinion.

· · ·

"We are more alike, my friends, than we are unalike."
-Maya Angelou-

· · ·

"We are very good at preparing to live, but not very good at living. We know how to sacrifice ten years for a diploma, and we are willing to work very hard to get a job, a car, a house and so on. But we have difficulty remembering that we are alive in the present moment, the only moment there is for us to be alive."
-Thich Nhat Hanh-

· · ·

So the other day we had a fourteen-year-old autistic boy who came to our house looking for friends because he didn't have any and told me he was bullied a lot. He walked all the way from near our old house, which is about a mile and a half or so away from where we live now. He knew his phone number, so after calling his mom, introducing myself, and letting her know he was here and safe, he proceeded to stay for a couple hours and play outside with my kids, a couple kids I baby sit, and my niece and nephew from next door. This kid was *so happy!* It tore my heart open when he told me he has no friends and he was bullied all the time, it really and truly did.

Before he went home, my amazing, big-hearted son gave the boy, Andrew, one of his favorite Nerf guns, a big Michelangelo action figure, a small Nerf gun, and a ton of bullets for the guns. No one asked him to do so. I beamed with pride and told him how proud I was of him.

Then I asked him why he gave away one of his favorite guns and other toys, and he looked right at me and said, "Mommy, I have *lots* of guns and toys. He has none. I want him to be happy like I am."

I swear to you, my heart swelled up so much with emotion it felt like it was going to burst.

My son, Jackson, is growing up to be such an amazing kid with a huge heart. Saying we're proud of our baby boy doesn't even come close to what we are. Next time we go shopping, he's getting the coolest, biggest Nerf gun we can find.

Adults, we can take lessons from children, as compassion and love come naturally to them. It's us who tarnish it.

•   •   •

Honestly, not much irrelevant bullshit gets to me anymore. It doesn't matter to me who believes that or not. Ever since my relapse last year (2018), the way I view myself and the world surrounding me has completely changed. I see a magic in it of which I was never previously aware. I have a peace and calmness in me I never knew to be possible, and I know a very large part of it has to do with my realization there is, in fact, something bigger than us all. Call it what you will. I choose to call it a God of my understanding and simply the universe itself. I can feel Him/It in me, and I am so, so grateful I was deemed "enough" to be part of a much bigger, incredible plan, despite my less-than-perfect past and the millions of mistakes I've made. For the first time in my life, I have no lasting fear, hate, anger, or animosity. No resentments, far less nightmares, and an overall understanding we are put on this earth to make it a better place and to love the people surrounding us, no matter our differences, to embrace all as humanity, as fellow human beings. People are not meant to be alone. We are not solitary beings meant to live life separately. We are built at our cores, for love, for compassion, and for understanding. We are meant to inevitably die surrounded by our loved ones, not regretting a single thing from this roller coaster we call life.

That being said, I wish with all my heart I knew where we went wrong.

Take a look at the world we live in. We are, piece-by-piece, burning it to the ground. All the hate, the racism and fear. The judgment and condemning of others based on our own ideas of what should be, instead of what actually is. When will enough be enough? When there's nothing left to destroy?

Change, quite literally, comes from within, and it starts with each and every one of us as individuals, and until you have achieved peace in your own heart and soul, you don't have any right to judge another human being, simple as that.

•　　•　　•

Well slap me silly and call me Sally, Mercedes has three e's in it, and they're all pronounced differently.

•　　•　　•

Let me set the scene for you:

Twas a beautiful day, with the sun shining brightly and the birds chirping sweetly. I decided to buy one of those KISS do-it-yourself gel nail kits, as I don't have a lot of free time to go get them done professionally. I was excited! I'd get to be a lady and shit because I am nothing if not classy.

With my son at school, I got my precious daughter comfy on the couch with a granola bar and Paw Patrol and headed to the kitchen where I was going to do my nails. Being graceful and elegant is not my strong suit, so I began having trouble with the glue almost immediately. Sure as shit, I somehow managed to not only glue my left thumb to my pointer finger, but also the tube of glue itself to my palm. Then, I heard a loud BANG followed by the distinct sound of my daughter running (she's two but sounds like a grown ass man when she runs). I shoot up and immediately head to the living room and discover the source of the sound. She had flipped her toy chest over.

Annoyed with my fingers still glued together and the tube riding along on my hand, I headed toward the basement, which is to where I heard her take off. I took no more than three steps before she rounded the corner, shot up past me, knocking me on this sweet ass while twisting my ankle and busting my shin. Today was *not* going to be the day a *toddler* gets the best of me I decided, so I got up, wounded and stuck together, and moved forward. It was quiet, serene…almost *too* quiet…the type of quiet that happens right before *it* happens, know what I mean? I don't see or hear her immediately, which puts me on the defense right away. An unseen enemy is a dangerous enemy. I check the bathroom—nope. The kid's room—nope. The kitchen—nope. Then I headed to the living room where it all began…and I found her…found her sitting on the couch, balls deep in a package of soft and chewy chocolate chip cookies, underneath her favorite blanket, watching Paw Patrol, and looking at me with this stunned look like she couldn't fathom there being any logical reason for me to be standing in the doorway with blood dripping down my leg, fingers glued the fuck together, and sweat pouring down my face.

I'm now sitting outside smoking a cigarette, certain I lost to something somehow, but not certain what. All I know is my two-year-old daughter outsmarted me for some cookies.

• • •

Are we done yet? Keeping petty hate and racism alive? We have a nineteen-year-old woman, Marlen Ochoa-Uriostegui, who's baby was cut out of her, *cut out of her*, by demons. We have a little boy, A.J. Freund, murdered by his parents and buried in a field; a little girl, Semaj Crosby, whose body was shoved under a couch and asphyxiated, and hundreds of other children dead with DCFS involvement…You know, the agency that's supposed to help protect and save our babies. Semaj was murdered two years ago, and no charges have been filed. I'm still waiting for the monster that shot Dijon Walker a.k.a. Chase to be caught, the little boy who took a bullet in a drive-by this past February 2019. Kids are going missing every day. Women are going missing every day. My friend, Adam Furtick's, murderer is still out there. He'll be gone two years this October 2019. Maleah Davis is still missing in Houston, with her step-father as the prime suspect. Zoey Pereira was burned to death in a car she was chained in so she couldn't escape by her father, her own father. We have a monster that woke up wanting to kill someone, so he picked up an innocent five-year-old boy and threw him over a balcony at the mall, just because. How many kids have we lost to suicide this year? How many school shootings? We have an opioid epidemic rampaging through our streets. There are, as of now May 2019, 161 documented homicides in Chicago so far this year.

Make no mistake, these are not human beings committing these atrocious acts against our loved ones. Opioids are not just pills or heroin. These are demons in their purest form. We need to stop focusing our attention on hating one another, and come together to defeat our real problems, our real issues. Fuck this divide. We are all the same. We're all human beings that bleed red, and we are all suffering in some way from a monster that lives and breathes here on Earth. Just because it may not be the same monster as yours doesn't mean you can't empathize with someone else's and do what you can to help them. I'm so heartsick today, and so frustrated with all the hate surrounding us. If we want change, we need to be the change. God never said the weapons wouldn't form, He said they wouldn't prosper, so put the ugly words and actions down, and be love instead of hate. Our world needs it right now, badly, and it's up to us to fix this broken thing, that simple.

•   •   •

My girlfriend called me up, asking me if I wanted to go running with her.

Lolololololllll.

Negative, Ghost Rider, I have a date to eat my weight in Cheez Whiz (or snake cheese, as my daughter calls it).

•   •   •

"Be the person who cares. Be the person who makes an effort, who loves without hesitation. Be the person who makes people feel seen. There is nothing stronger than someone who continues to stay soft in a world that hasn't always been kind to them."

-tinybuddism.com-

Absolutely. Make it a point to help, or even just compliment, at least one complete stranger a day, and see how quickly your own life will become flooded with love. That one small gesture of kindness may be the reason someone doesn't put a bullet in their head, and the world needs more of that.

•   •   •

Taking a stroll with Annabel:

walks past two ladies

Me: silence
Annabel: I am not a jerk, Mommy!
Two ladies: *both stare at me like I'm an asshole*
Me: What the fuck?
Annabel: *laughs like a psychopath and tells me she loves me*

•   •   •

One of the most important realizations I have come to is that most, if not all, of my defense mechanisms I had derived previously to survive were now creating turmoil in my life. Your brain's natural instinct is to protect you at any cost, so yes, the walls and whatnot I had built around my mind up to a certain point had served me well in aiding in my well-being. They were there to block out or lock away anything that could or would cause me pain or anguish.

But I had, at long last, reached the point in my life where I realized keeping people out was doing harm to me in every sense of the word. I needed to let people in because I needed help. I needed support. I needed to trust, to love, and to allow myself to be loved. Can't do that if your heart is surrounded by a fortress. The habits you create to survive will no longer serve you when it's time to thrive. You need to get yourself out of survival mode. New habits, new life, baby! There's no easy way to start, no right way. You just open up. If you get hurt or let down in the process, it's okay. Keep going, *do not* give up or give in. That's how they win, your demons. Learn from the experience and keep it moving forward, but please know the lesson is 100 percent *never* to give up on people, to not trust anyone, or that you are alone, *never*. It's just showing you who *isn't* for you to make room for the people in your life who are.

• • •

Man, I lost today. The Devil won, no doubt about it. I'm still not certain even what pulled me into the funk I'm in, really, but I have been in a shit mood since my feet hit the floor. It's gloomy as Hell outside too. That certainly didn't help things.

Here's the difference between my mindset now, and what I would've been like a couple years ago. While yeah, it has definitely been a crap day, I'm not letting it ruin me inside. I accepted the day for what it was: pure shit. I allowed the unpleasant feelings to be felt and tried to understand their origin, but never once did I let them overpower me. This is how I win. This is how *you* win. By fighting the feelings, you just give them power. Allow them to come, just control where they travel. The only way out is through, I've learned. Negative emotions have just as much a right to be here as the positive ones because without them there would be no balance. I had to learn to show respect to them in a sense, but make no mistake, I am the sole person responsible for my actions and reactions to my feelings and emotions, so sure, I had a bad day, but I'm thankful for the struggles from this one because I'll be that much more appreciative when tomorrow comes. He won the battle, but I win the war, and that's what counts.

• • •

"He who blames others has a long way to go on his journey. He who blames himself is halfway there. He who blames no one has arrived."

-Chinese Proverb-

• • •

I could've focused the majority of my time detailing every horrific account of every bad thing I've been through, or every bad thing I've done in this book. As a matter of fact, the first couple attempts at it pretty much did, but I decided not to do that because it would be detrimental to me trying to bring you hope. It's not that the details surrounding the negative points in life aren't meaningful or shouldn't be shared at all, quite the contrary. It is so important to share your stories, your struggles, with others. Your story could be the one that opens a person's eyes to the fact they're not alone. It's just that the negative aspects in your life shouldn't be the focal point of it. Accept the negative points. Share them. Tell them, but also speak on how you're blessed. How you *survived*. How you got through it, or how you're getting through it. Share your sorrows, your fears, your struggles, but then share your joys, your happiness, and your laughter. Share your hugs and your smiles. You are not perfect, and that's exactly what makes you perfect. And the world needs you just as you are.

You are not alone. Ever. If you ever feel you are, my email is enclosed in this book. Write me, I *will* write you back. In prison, at home, I don't care where. Thank you for reading this and for being a part of my journey moving forward.

atomasino85@gmail.com